look i bought plants

Library of Congress Cataloging-in-Publication Data

Names: Garron, Taylor, author. | Victor, Eva, author.
Title: Look I bought plants : and other poems about life and stuff / by Taylor Garron and Eva Victor.
Description: San Francisco : Chronicle Books, [2021]
Identifiers: LCCN 2020041653 | ISBN 9781797210148 (paperback)
Subjects: LCGFT: Poetry.
Classification: LCC PS3607.A7745 L66 2021 | DDC 811/.6--dc23
LC record available at https://lccn.loc.gov/2020041653
Manufactured in China.

Design by AJ Hansen & Maggie Edelman.

10 9 8 7 6 5 4 3 2 1

Chronicle Books LLC
680 Second Street
San Francisco, CA 94107
www.chroniclebooks.com

look
i bought plants

And Other Poems about Life and Stuff

By Taylor Garron and Eva Victor

CHRONICLE BOOKS

SAN FRANCISCO

contents

i will venmo you, she said
she never did

the moment i began
to kind of like my face
is the same moment i began
to kind of loathe my body
because my higher power knew
that i would
not
act
right
if i was confident in both
at
the
same
time
and that is how i know
god is a woman

i don't fit into last summer's swim suit
woe
is
me
but it's because i am getting thicc
so i guess that's fine

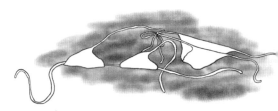

the imminent environmental collapse
means i will not have the opportunity to
bear children
and that's pretty sick, honestly
pregnancy freaks me out

there is a full-length
head hair
stuck in my
butt crack

i am choosing to ignore it

i love this new miniskirt
i impulse bought
even though it immediately
brings up
a flood of questions
about
my gender
identity

returning
it

exercise?
no

i have been catcalled
in a full winter coat
in a blizzard
i have been catcalled
while sobbing outside of an Urban Outfitters
while throwing up outside of a bar
i have been catcalled
walking with a man
walking with a child
walking with purpose
i have been catcalled many times
it has never been from someone hot

i should get a Fitbit
But i will look stupid with a Fitbit
So Maybe
i will just stay on my couch forever

this coffee tastes
like you made it wrong
and yet
i will not say a word

oh my god
i am so so sorry
i forgot to answer this email
it must have slipped my mind
because
i hate you

look
i bought plants
my life is the same
i have not matured in any way
but now
there are some leaves in my room

i will eat a salad for lunch each day
i will eat a pint of ice cream for dinner each night
this is balance

i am ever-changing
i will never stop growing
i am becoming the woman i want to be
the only thing that stays the same is
i will never

       ever

         order a salad

you should wear a helmet
even though
it looks fucking dumb

ah
what a beautiful world it is
the birds are chirping
the sun is shining
i will be
the first 45 year old woman
with acne

why
would
i
ever
for any reason
professional or personal
leave
my bed?

happy birthday
you say

easier said
than done

my roommate is
having
sex
good
for
her
i
guess

i am watching
F R I E N D S
this is a
C R Y
F O R
H E L P

should i get bangs
or process my emotions
of disappointment
about where i am in my
life right now

it's the afternoon
oh how time passes
while i am
watching
TV

i have to pee
and yet
i will never
go

i am so so sorry
and i know this makes me sound
insane
but
and i'm sorry again for asking
but would it be cool
if i made a liveable wage?
no worries if not
after all
i know this is selfish
of me

wearing a dress
makes me feel
like a boy
and that's
that on that

i want a dog
but one that
does not
poop

bought a bookshelf
like a good grown up
but i only have
seven books
you can never
win

you found my nudes?
fine
you found the 600 photos it took
to get the shot?
not fine

find me a beautiful lake
to swim in
find me a cozy cabin
to sleep in
find me a delicious dinner
to feast on
don't worry
i'll find something
to complain about

my period
connects me
to my womanhood
also
it justifies the moments
i feel the urge
to kill someone for doing something
lightly annoying
like humming in public
or standing just a hair too close to me
or being happy with someone they love

flowers
are beautiful and live a short life
i
am beautiful only sometimes
and we actually don't know how long my life wil
something to
think about

as i sit on the couch
drinking Diet Coke
i wonder
will i achieve my dreams

doing laundry
can really remind a person
they are
fucking disgusting

why my underwear
have that on it
after only
three hours

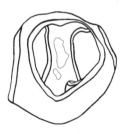

i do not remember
even one birthday party i had
before the age of 18
please do not
tell my mother

every day
my body
looks different
how
thrilling
for me

i never owned Converse Chuck Taylor All Stars
where do i pick up
my prize

thinking about drinking water
now
THAT'S
how an adult
does
life

when you pour a little wine
in the glass
and i swoosh it
then smell it
i hope you know
i am doing that
for you

do not confuse me with generation z
i am youthful, yet millennial
i know nothing of tiktok

i am turning into my mother
which is to say
that i am starting to hate my father

do i drink water?
what am i, a peasant?
i'm a seltzer bitch

hulu
burrito
prosecco

my hierarchy of needs

i don't think these edibles are working
i shall eat another

oh
no

goodnight my someone
goodnight my love
a song i sing
to the seltzer i keep by my bed
that i will not sip throughout the night
and will inevitably be
flat when i wake up
despite my best intentions

i have failed myself
by never wearing fake lashes before this
moment
just childish of me

i never feel more sexually empowered
than when i am wearing an olive green
beanie

i will not explain further

oh
you don't tip your baristas
i shall fetch the guillotine

i will cure my uti
by just drinking water
and cranberry juice

this has never worked before
but it probably will this time

i am pretending to be disgusted
by zit popping videos
but again, i am pretending

should
i
get
a
juul
?

do i need another tattoo
or a retirement fund
who is to say

i went to a clothing swap
with my canvas tote
which is to say
i am a climate activist

why yes
i did spend thirty dollars on this matte
lipstick
which i will wear once
and never again

drunk at the grocery store
f u c k
y e a h

leggings count as pants
no further questions

if i buy more Glossier
will i be a better person?
or just an almost imperceptibly better
looking one?
remains to be seen

could you make me a mocktail?
and while you're at it
here is my dignity

do i want you
to bring me back a snack from the store?
stupid question
and furthermore
yes

in many ways
i am a foodie
actually only in one way
and that way is
frozen Trader Joe's taquitos

i will take one puff of this joint
and then have a mild panic attack
hope that's chill

my vagina
smells
off

hm

should i become a stripper?
ha
as if i possess even a fraction of the core
strength necessary

got a membership at my local gym

now what?

i am clinically depressed
but yes, you're right
perhaps a walk in the sun
will fix the chemical imbalance in my
brain

you just walked into me
i will apologize profusely

friendship

didn't you wear that yesterday? she asked
keep your damn voice down, i said

sorry
why would i hang out with you
when i can
hang out with
my best friend
and talk about you?

a friend is
someone who orders a big pizza even
though you said
none for me
a friend is
someone who offers to kill your ex every
day until you
feel better
a friend is
someone who pretends to like a bad band
so you don't feel
as lonely in your
bad taste

my cell phone rings
who could be calling
at this hour
or any hour
what the fuck is wrong with you
text me bitch

do you like this shirt?

k you hesitated
i am returning it

i want my friend's boobs
she wants mine
it is the patriarchy

it is crucial
c r u c i a l
that women stick together

except for that one
who keeps looking at my crush
she unfortunately must die

this group chat is Not Fun
yet Here I Am

you are crying
over a guy
who doesn't deserve to even look at you
and kinda stinks

i will give you advice
which you will promptly ignore
and sleep with him again
even though he kinda stinks

the cycle will repeat
ad infinitum
until you find a different guy
who probably also stinks

friendship is a flat circle

ah
big sports game
yay
i
cannot
wait
for it all to happen

oh
you're asking
if you can say something?
well now that you've asked
it's actually gonna be a huge no
for me

if i say
hahahahah
this conversation
is
frankly
Over

what's your eta
just curious
how late you will think i am

CAPS LOCK
OR ANGRY
OR
BOTH

let's go out
get dressed up
do our makeup
make a real night of it

or more realistically

let's say we will do that
and then lose steam
and end up at mine
eating pad see ew

my optometrist
told me
i can't come back
until i
take an anti-anxiety medication
but congratulations on your engagement

should i get a septum piercing
or should i stop asking people
if i should
get a septum piercing

congratulations on your
fancy car
i would rather spend
$14
on a breakfast burrito
every morning
for the rest of my life

god made us different clothing and shoe sizes
because we would stunt too hard
if our wardrobes were interchangeable

a blessing in disguise

the girls in the
fuzzy North Face jackets
haunt me

in my nightmares
they do not see me
they do not hear me
they do not even hate me
they're just
standing there
together

LOOK I BOUGHT PLANTS

hm
why do the pants look so good on her
and so bad
on me
because of this
i will not sleep tonight

my friend deserves the world
i deserve nothing
and she would say
the same about
herself

having a sister means never having to say
you're sorry
except in this moment, when you've
ruined my fav top
bitch

if you like my outfit
you have to tell me
that's the law

you have had a trust fund?
this whole time?
that feels deceptive

sweet friend
you hover above public toilet seats
but fuck strangers with no protection

sweet friend
i urge you
to examine your priorities

beautiful woman

do i want to be your best friend?
or am i incredibly attracted to you?
my catholic upbringing will never allow
me to know

it is evident that
my roommate is eating my frozen pierogies
i will seethe silently
and purchase more pierogies

if you've seen at least one of my nipples
we are best friends

i do not like my friend's boyfriend
but i do like my friend
a
predicament

every single one of my friends is so beautiful
those odds seem astronomical
and yet

"girl"
she texted me
as i readied myself
for the forthcoming goss

you can tell me your secrets
they are safe with me
i will tell no one
(except my best friend)

i know you are my friend
because
when i tell you i hate my boobs
you tell me to
shut the fuck up
and you say
in a very mean way
"your boobs are perfect"

you are lactose intolerant
yet
here we sit
housing an order of mozz sticks

i admire this about you

my best friend is a guy
it's easy
it's possible
me?
i'm a guy's girl
guys just
make sense to me
i love their brains

-   no one ever

another high school friend is pregnant
another baby named jayden

let's go out!
let's get drunk!
let's share childhood traumas!

only if you want though

dating

Love
    Is
        So
            Bad

wait
remind me where we met
was it tinder?
okcupid?
hinge?
bumble?
oh
oh
you're ghosting me anyway

eye contact? nah
a coy smile? nope
asking his name? hell no
i will only think strongly in his direction

you are not my boyfriend
and i, not your girlfriend
we only fuck
and get dinner
and meet each others' friends
and plus one to weddings
and talk about the future
and drunkenly name hypothetical children

nothing serious.

We can split
this
Oh okay, are you
sure?
Well, thank
you
and (more quietly) thank
god.

you've never dated
a non-white person
and it shows

young man
do not speak to me
or look at me
or breathe my air
unless you are prepared to get me pregnant
immediately

your apartment smells like cat
i am willing to look past it
because you
are good
at fuck

i've had pedicures
that have lasted longer than
our boring relationship

i want to fall in love
deeply in love
with someone who is okay
with not being my first priority
or even the second or third
i want a lover i don't have to love
and maybe who listens to bright eyes

big dick, but no rhythm
it's long, but not thick
a
pen
cil
but at least
he'll eat me out

i can tell
you don't wash
your towels

do not be embarrassed
that you came quickly
seriously!
you are only human
i am empathetic
and also
i'm pretty tired

my desire for you was dashed to bits
when i met your roommate
who was objectively hotter

Sex with women
Is much more nerve-wracking
Than getting
Dumb
Dick

please
sir
let me ghost you in peace

If by the time I count to 10 he does not text back
We will never have a baby named Ashlyn

i like focaccia more than
any man
i've ever met

if you had sex with someone before we
started dating
i'm sorry but
i deserve better

can you find it in your heart
to forgive me
for doing what i did
when what i did
was have a big perfect ass

flowers and chocolate are stupid
but
i want them

i want you to want me

that's me
asking the barista at my coffee shop
to care back

my boyfriend says
he's 30 and has it together
but sometimes
i feel
he is 17
and actually
does not have it together

i am horny
and i WILL
let the lack of sex i am having
stop me
from enjoying my life

C
A
L
M

D
O
W
N

says a man

i care not
whether he lives or dies

i think about
Double Stuf Oreos
far too much

more
than any person
i have ever slept with

i am mad at you
but
i will never say

you see
it's just easier this way
give it ten years
by then
i will probably
have killed you

oh
good morning
how did you sleep
your face is less good today
and that is something i will
keep to myself

yes i will get naked!

well

here's my body

so

the greatest joy of
my life
is watching
you
play guitar badly

Great...

if you say you love my butt
then i am happy
and also
congratulations!!
you have the opportunity to
ruin my life

tell me you love me
but let me warn you
when you do
i will freak out

oh and just like that
you're showing me
your favorite
Rick and Morty episode

every time i've ever 69'd someone
i hold back laughter
please,
to former lovers reading this:
forgive me

my ex
left a drill at my apartment
should i text?
"hi!
you'll need to buy a new drill
i broke yours
not on purpose
also
how is
your sister?"

if you wear a baseball cap
i will unfortunately
try to fuck you
if you take it off
i will want to fuck you less
so
keep that in mind

why are you confused?
all i want is for you to
compliment my body
without reminding me
of societal pressures
to look a certain way
while also objectifying me
but in a hot way
not a condescending way

i am not in a place where i can be in a
relationsh--
oh
look at that
i am in love with you

men
turn 30
and
go crazy

you know i am a
woman for the people
because
even i say
tip your bartenders
and that includes my ex
who is now a bartender

before i cum
i love your beard
after i cum
i want to rip it off your face
every day
i stray further and further
from
heterosexuality

the way
the boy
eats the burger
with reckless abandon
turns me on
but i will never
tell a soul
oh look
onion
still
falling
out his mouth

pretending to fall asleep
so i can hear you whisper the words
"i love you"
before you are ready to say them to me

dear the man who is
mad at me in my direct message folder
i am sorry
i made you sad
i owe you an explanation
and a sexual favor
apparently

how is
Jacob from middle school?
i hope he
regrets
letting me go
(to be clear
i never told him
i had a crush
on him)

i love Cheez-Its more consistently
than any man i've ever seen naked

what i want— partner who loves and
respects me
what i have— dude who calls me for sex
once weekly

i suppose this will do for now

if you laugh at my joke
s u r p r i s e !
we're dating now

you look so hot with glasses
you look so hot with a beard
i find you kind of generally hot
which is a mental and emotional burden

my love language is
words of affirmation
but that does not mean
i will not accept
gifts

i am drinking this beer
despite not liking beer
to me this is worth it
because i want to impress you
because the sides of your hair are greying

i left my first love years ago
and by first love
i mean dark rum

a man with dimples?
unfair to my reproductive system

why would i buy weed
when i could simply sleep with a weed
dealer
that's called working smarter
not harder

oh, you're non-monogamous?
i love that for you
leave me alone

what if we went camping
what if we got married
what if we had a baby

haha, just kidding!
what if we went camping

you are either good at going down on me
or good at giving me money
you cannot be neither

you also can be both, if you want
your decision

don't look at me like that
i'll get pregnant right now
don't test me

oh to be ghosted
when you were planning on ghosting
a treat

oh
you prefer brunettes?
even the non-white ones?

oh
you have gone silent

you're not very funny
you're not very cute
i'm not very interested in you

i was bored on tinder one day
and now, here we are

have you ever considered
treating me as though i am a human
with feelings
and boundaries
worthy of respect?

no pressure, of course
we're just fuck buddies

walk of *shame*?
more like
walk of *just came**!

*pretended to cum

met a guy
at the vegan co-op
and before you ask
yes, he smelled

you don't know the difference
between a fruit roll-up and a fruit-by-the-foot
you're too old for me sir

my kink
is mutually enjoyable sex

do not shame me

i need a little dick in my life
and to be clear
i'm using that adjective to mean quantity

this relationship
is on thin ice
so yes
i will accept this broadway show and
gourmet dinner as a date
it's the least you can do

...and every other

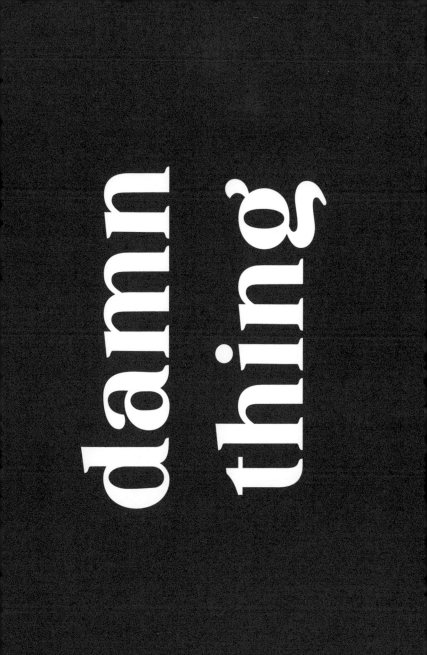

damn thing

i am a gemini
sorry

Do I want to hear your new single?
No
Never
Would rather
Eat my own hand

Moon in Aquarius
Jupiter in Scorpio
Mars in Pisces
Why won't my boyfriend
Grab my
Huge Ass

postmates checks in
before
during
and the next morning
ah,
i have found him
my dream man

my ancestors immigrated to a place
they didn't know
they struggled

for me
to be able
to smoke pot every day

in a beautiful twist
nobody gets me

oh you work out
Congratulations
do you want me to
throw you
a party?

O Moon
Stop trying to tell me
I am a
Boring Lover

do i want you to cut my cuticles
i have no idea
what that means
do you have a pro con list
i can consult

dogs?

better
than
people

no
exceptions

!

do

minions

fuck

oh no
my phone is dead
how did that happen
you don't think
no
it can't be
because i'm on it
every hour
of every day?

i would rather die
than have someone give me
mouth to mouth resuscitation

i actually
do not care
whether you
do or don't
find what you're
looking for

i can feel so alone
in a crowd of people
i can feel so found
in a bite of meatball sub

oh it's raining
finally
the sky is as depressed
as i am

Diet Coke
water for women on the go

if i was a pirate
and they were like
"we need you up on the deck
there's a storm
come on"
i'd be like,
"sorry,
i am just not feeling it
today
good luck
tho
seriously"

whenever a woman says
"i am a witch"
i think
no you are not
you are a girl from
Maine
who went to
Oberlin and realized she's
a little gay
but not enough to
feel it makes sense to
tell her family

oh my makeup?
just a sweep of mascara
a smudge of chapstick
and the clear, dewy skin of someone who
is pretending
that climate change doesn't exist

i saw you
across the vegan restaurant
what was that you were eating?
it looked good

if i had money
i would still be depressed
but at least
i could indulge in
purchasing
this eucalyptus oil i've had my eye on
for quite some time

little kid shoe
by side of road
not gonna let my brain
run too wild
with this

a pigeon just flew
too close
to my face
should i write a book about
that experience

this woman
in my spin class
is dancing
too hard
what if she hurts herself?
wow
cannot believe
i also
paid for this class

do you like buffets?
do you like foodborne illness?
this is the same question

i'd like
an iced latte
single shot
light ice
yes
i want to pay six dollars
for a cup of milk

wow this museum
has art in it
and i am looking at it
still

yes
give me a moment
to find a pen
to write down the phone number
because apparently
this is the
Middle Ages

cheese
not enough
ever

hello
Shark Tank:
so it's
a museum
but i'm still in bed

the girl with the dragon tattoo
has nothing on
the girl with the treble clef tattoo she got
the moment she turned
18

my mom spent time in France
because of this
it is honest of me when i say
i am
French

do AirPods look
this
fucking dumb
on everyone

stop making movies
with problematic men
you cowards

never

enough

pasta

never

enough

pizza

always

too

much

spinach

and so on

and so forth

kids
musn't
have
bangs
if your kid has bangs
this is a poem
for you

i wonder what my AirPods
talk about when
i close
the box

oh no
it's Christmas
time to scurry around
looking for a
World War II book
for my dad
that he has surely already
read and
hated

long hair?
i look like a horse
short hair?
i look like my 4th grade teacher Karen
who made us stay in the room while a kid
shit his pants
as to not make him feel bad

when Tyra Banks
yelled
at that girl
that was
inappropriate

i wonder what they mean
when they say
Toyota
Camry

whenever i sing
it sounds
less good
than i would like

Hey There Delilah
was not
that good
of a song

who said
there should be
garnish
ever

do i have enough pairs of black ankle
booties?
probably
will i buy this pair regardless?
definitely

thank you for this necklace!
i love it!

(i do not)

i have chosen
a new god
and her name is
queso

my Asos package has been delivered
i am forced to survive for at least another
day
damn it!
and at the same time
sick!

my birthday is this month
which is to say
my birthday is today

why are you worried about me?
do not be concerned
i am simply
experimenting with berets

i will hold in this sneeze
until my head explodes
i am a lady

i am sad
so i will listen to sad music
to feel sadder
that is my right